Practitioners Guide

to Evidence Based Golf Psychology

Practitioners Guide

to Evidence Based Golf Psychology

by

Dr John Pates

The British Institute of Golf Psychology

Published by Ex-L-Ence Publishing a division of Winghigh Limited, Gloucester, England.

www.ex-l-ence.com

ISBN 978-1-909133-06-8

About the Author

John has over 8 years of applied experience working on the European Golf Tour. He has worked with 3 Major Winners, 8 Ryder cup players and over 15 European Tour winners. He has also provided mental training for 3 world champions and 5 winners on the challenge and senior tour. Taken together, John has worked with over 50 tour players and has coached golfers to win European, World, and Ryder Cup events.

Inspired by positive psychologists, John was the first researcher to publish empirical data on the client-centered approach and the positive effects of hypnosis in golf. John has also published two books and has over 20 academic publications. He is one of the world's leaders in developing optimal performance environments for elite golfers, and he currently manages a team of world-class coaches and sports science practitioners at the University of Derby in the UK.

The British Institute of Golf Psychology was founded by John in 2012. The aim of the institute is to inform coaches, psychologists, and golfers about evidence-based Golf Psychology. The institute also aims to provide courses that will become the standard training for practitioners working in the golf profession. John uses cutting edge approaches to training, often delivered via one to one teaching. He also tailors each session to the needs and strengths of the client. The most important feature of this training programme is its emphasis on research and empirical evidence-based data.

Table of Contents

Introduction 1

Building Bridges 2

Unconscious Rapport Building Techniques 3

Assessing Performance Potential 7

Defining the Outcomes from your Session 10

A Client Centered Approach 12

Ideal Performance Qualities 13

The Psychological Skills Questionnaire 14

Emotions in Sport 16

The Optimal Performance Emotion Profile 17

Positive Emotions 23

General Happiness Scale 24

Satisfaction with Life Scale 25

The Optimism Survey 26

The Power of Confidence 27

The Self-Confidence Survey 29

The Power of Inspiration 31

The Inspiration Skills Survey 32

The Skills of an Inspirational Player 35

Peak Performance 36

The Wheel of Peak Performance 37

Mental Toughness 38

The Wheel of Mental Toughness 39

The Successful Mindset Survey 40

Strength-Based Approach 42

Attitudes and Beliefs 44

Attitudes 48

The Function of Attitudes 49

Attitude Advice from the Greats 51

Positive Attitudes for Golfers 53

Goal Setting 54

A Case Study 58

How I work with Elite Golfers 65

Imagery 69

Imagery Techniques 74

Other Performance Enhancing Imagery Techniques 75

The Swish Technique 77

Self-Talk 79

Guidelines about Self-Talk 83

Concentration 85

Pre-shot and Post-shot Routines 86

Music as an Intervention 87

Autotelic States as an Intervention 88

Further Action 89

Introduction

In the world of competitive golf the difference between winning and losing often comes down to psychological variables such as attitudes, beliefs and mental skills. Over the past 30 years chartered psychologists have discovered there are a number of psychological strategies that can be used to optimize a golfers performance. The practitioners guide will teach you the strategies used by psychologists working with elite golfers.

The guide also provides practitioners with a comprehensive communication and profiling system that identifies the strengths, skills and needs of golfers playing in competitive environments. The consultancy approach highlighted in the guide are strength-based and client-centered. Both methods are known to maximize the performance of golfers.

The guide also offers practitioners a number of intervention strategies. The interventions are used on the European Golf Tour by chartered golf psychologists and are specifically designed to help golfers improve their performances and trigger mental states such as flow and the zone.

Taken together, the content of this guide has been used to help golfers win Majors, World titles and European tour events.

Follow the guide and help your players reach their performance potential.

Building Bridges

When you meet a client for the first time you need to make them feel comfortable and at ease. Always meet in a comfortable warm place and begin developing rapport by asking open-ended questions. Open-ended questions cannot be answered with a 'yes' and 'no'. They usually start with who, what, where, how when.

Here are some examples:

"How did you come to hear about me?"

"What made you come and see me?"

"Where is your game at the moment?"

"When did you decide to come and see me?"

"Who are the people you train with?"

Good rapport building will stimulate conversations and develop trust between you and your client. The more trust you develop, the more likely your client will disclose to you their personal information. It will then make it easier for the client to disclose to you the reason why they are coming to see you. Allowing the client to set the pace of the session will also develop trust and rapport.

Yet another way to develop trust is to share some personal experiences in an informal and friendly way. Never talk about personal problems but you can share personal stories or strategies that will increase the client's confidence in you helping them. I always find a story about working on the European Golf Tour really helps build rapport and the confidence the client needs in you, for you to do good work.

Unconscious Rapport Building Techniques

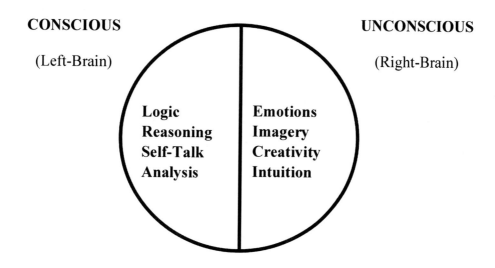

CONSCIOUS

(Left-Brain)

Logic
Reasoning
Self-Talk
Analysis

UNCONSCIOUS

(Right-Brain)

Emotions
Imagery
Creativity
Intuition

Psychologists who analyze nonverbal behaviour will tell you that people who get on with each other will tend to mirror and match each other's body language at a unconscious level. Deliberate matching and mirroring by you, the practitioner, is a way you can communicate without saying a thing. There are two types of non-verbal matching techniques you can use to build rapport at an unconscious level.

1. Mirroring: here the practitioner deliberately and identically adopts every posture and movement made by the client. When you use this technique you should match the client's movements as if your body is their reflection in a mirror. This is useful for stationary postures only and should be avoided if your client is constantly moving.

2. Cross matching: here the practitioner matches a certain aspect of the client's behavior with a totally different body part. For example, you could match their breathing by swinging your leg in rhythm with the client's breath.

You can practice matching and mirroring using the following exercise.

Exercise

Choose a partner and hold a conversation during which each of you speaks for a few minutes on several occasions. Take it in turn to speak. The 'listener' mirrors all of the postures made by the 'speaker'. Each takes it in turn to be the listener. Both partners should make a mental note of the feelings and the qualities during the exchange of communication.

Take a few minutes to share experiences at the end of the exercise.

Repeat this process, however this time the listener should deliberately mismatch all of the speaker's postures. Take it in turns and give each other feedback. Play with the exercise, try to deliberately mismatch posture during the discussion.

In consultancy you should attempt to match the client as much as possible. This should continue throughout the consultancy process until the end of the session. Below are other ways you can match your client's behaviour. You will notice the techniques described above and below are mostly designed to communicate with the unconscious part of the client.

Breathing in Harmony

Pay attention to your client's breathing. By matching the breathing of your client you will maintain a deep level of communication with your client, creating a sub-conscious sense of 'harmony'. By matching the breathing in this way you can start to slow down your client's breathing.

This indirectly helps them to relax. Matching a client's breathing in this way is essential when inducing a hypnotic trance.

Talking Back

In addition to matching posture you can also match the voice of your client. Matching the voice tonality, tempo, pitch and volume of the client serves the same purpose as matching the breathing.

Matching Predicates

Similarly client's can feel safer and more comfortable if you can match the words they use to describe their sensory world. These words are called predicates. Some psychologists believe the words people use to describe their world shows a person dominant sensory system. Although there is no evidence for this conjecture matching peoples predicate-based statements will have a great rapport building effect.

Below are examples of predicate-based statements people often use.

Visual:

"It looks good to me".

"I can picture it".

"From my perspective".

Auditory:

"It sounds good".

"It's as clear as a bell".

"I ask myself".

Kinaesthetic:

"It feels right to me".

"I can handle it".

"I am under pressure".

Here are some other examples of sensory based predicates in visual, auditory and kinaesthetic systems.

VISUAL:

See, Picture, Imagine, Bright, Sparkling, Perceive, View, Focus, Shimmering, Clear, Clarify, Hazy, Blurred, Bleak, Dull, Image, Misty, Fuzzy, Foggy, Speculative, Hue, Hindsight, Obscure, Reveal, Panoramic, Magnify, Glassy, Huge, Minute, Steamy, Colour, Dim, Shady, Cloudy, Stormy, Precipitous, Distant, Brilliant, Radiant, Blinkered, Blindfolded, Gloom, Doom, Starry-eyed, Tunnel-vision, Outlook, Transparent, Translucent, Opaque, Fluorescent, Glaze, Small, Big, Glimmer, Rainbow.

AUDITORY:

Hear, Sound, Pitch, Tone, Volume, Noisy, Buzz, Raucous, Ringing, Loud, Soft, Listening, Whisper, Speak, Whistle, Hum, Drumming, Bell, Rattle, Song, Lilt, Band, Music, Orchestrate, Crescendo, Crashing, Musical, Harmony, Still, Echo, Rustle, Resonate, Twang, Jingle, Jangle, Clatter, Pitter-patter, Chord, Amplify, Scream, Bellow, Roar, Screech, Yell, Squeal, Silence, Thunder, Drone, Reverberate, Discord, On the wavelength, Click, Clear, Bang, Beat the Drum, Tune in, Fade, Note, Rhythm, Whisper, Crack, Moan, Clarity, Whine, Shriek, Quiet, Overtone.

KINAESTHETIC:

Feel, Pressure, Stress, Settled, At ease, Relaxed, Cushioned, High, Oppressed, Under the weather, Oh top of the world/things, Up in the air, Flat on the Floor, Down in the dumps, High as a kite, Ecstatic, Away with the fairies, Touched, Detached, Tired, Tread the boards carefully, Walking on eggshells, Delicate, Fragile, Robust, Determined, Fidgety, In bits, Hurt, Cold, Over the edge, Low, Sharp, Feel Beaten, Tender, Succulent, Soft, Clingy, Funny, Back to the wall, Burdened, Trapped, Hemmed in, Heavy handed, Swamped, Drowning, Dependent.

Assessing Performance Potential

After building rapport with your client you will need to ask your client questions about their performances. I am a positive psychologist so I like to ask questions around their strengths and best performances.

Every great performance has a beginning, middle and end and most of the time a client's best performances will have many performance enhancing triggers. Triggers may be certain thoughts, feeling, images, sounds or emotions that they experienced before the event or during the event. For example, when I worked with Graham McDowell and Darren Clarke they recalled that their best performances were often triggered by images of great shots, and thoughts that gave them inspiration.

If you ask client's to talk about their best performances you will learn to identify their 'performance enhancing triggers'. This line of questioning will give you valuable insights into how client's achieve optimal performance.

To help you gather this information use the following questions:

1. When did you first have an optimal performance experience?
2. How often does it happen?
3. How long does it last?
4. When does it not occur?
5. What other significant events in your life occurred at the same time as your greatest Moment?
6. What were your general beliefs about your self at the time of your best performance?
7. What were your family/life circumstances at the time of your best performance?
8. Tell me something about your best performances?
9. What did you think about during your best performance?
10. What were your feelings during your performance?
11. What emotions did you experience?

The last four questions in this list often give's me mixed results because some golfers have total recall of their peak performances and others can't remember a thing.

Golfers often cannot recall their peak performances because during a great performance they often enter a mental state described as 'the zone' or 'flow'.

Flow occurs when golfers stop 'conscious processing' (analysing their technique or the consequences of their behaviour during their performance). When golfers achieve this, they experience the holistic sensation of absorption and they act with total involvement. Other characteristics of flow are:

- The feeling that performance is effortless.
- Clear goals.
- Total concentration on task.
- Complete control without consciously doing so.
- No self-consciousness or evaluation.
- Time transformation, it is perceived as either speeding up or slowing down.
- An autotelic experience.

Neurological research evidence suggests when flow occurs the functions of the right hemisphere of the brain become activated and the corresponding functions of the left hemisphere of the brain become deactivated. The shift in consciousness from the left hemisphere (logical and analytical mode) to the right hemisphere (creative and intuitive) is thought to give better access to the functions of the brain which are important for good athletic performance. The diagram overleaf shows the functions of the cerebral hemispheres more clearly.

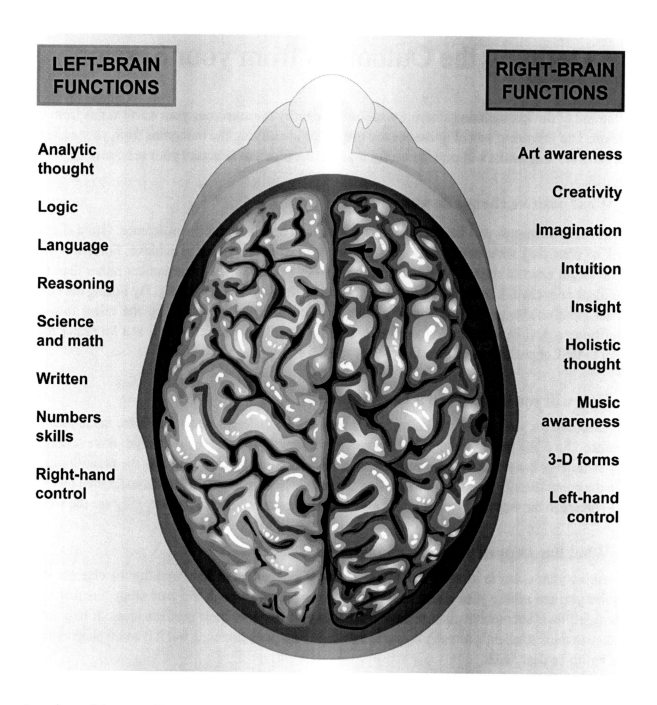

LEFT-BRAIN FUNCTIONS

Analytic thought

Logic

Language

Reasoning

Science and math

Written

Numbers skills

Right-hand control

RIGHT-BRAIN FUNCTIONS

Art awareness

Creativity

Imagination

Intuition

Insight

Holistic thought

Music awareness

3-D forms

Left-hand control

A review of the sport literature suggests we should be using interventions that access the functions of the right brain. This is why interventions such as imagery, hypnosis, music, positive statements and attitudes work.

Defining the Outcomes from your Session

At the end of the information gathering you should identify the outcomes your client wants from the session. The following sets of questions are useful for identifying the outcomes from your session. The answers they evoke will provide useful material on which to structure your sessions.

1. What positive change do you want?

When client's come to you for help they are not always certain about the outcomes. Often client's think of what they want to stop happening rather than what they want to achieve. For example, a golfer might want to control his nerves during the last stages of a big tournament rather than feel confident or excited. It is therefore important to frame the outcome positively. By asking the client "What positive change do you want?". When you do this you are directing the client towards identifying a positive outcome rather than a negative one. In my experience it is a lot easier for a client to look at positive outcomes rather than to look at stopping a behaviour.

2. How will you know when it has happened?

It is essential for your client's to know how things will be different when they have made positive changes. If a client makes changes yet has no way of identifying that these changes have occurred, they will never know that your techniques have worked. It is important for you, the practitioner, to help the client identify some way of knowing when they have reached their outcome. Often this will be a change in the way they feel. It might also be a change in attitude or the way they see the world.

3. What has stopped you from changing so far?

By asking your client to identify the things that have stopped them from making the changes they require you are asking your client to go on an inner search through the past strategies that have sabotaged their attempts to change their behaviour and improve their performances. It may seem strange to think of client's actually trying to sabotage their performances, but it is a real phenomenon that has to be dealt with.

When you ask "What has stopped you from changing so far?" the answer is rarely available at the conscious level. This is because answers of this nature are not in the client's conscious frames of reference. If they were already able to identify what has stopped them from changing so far they would have already made use of that information and started to change by themselves without intervention. The practitioner's role is to tease out the unconscious processes that lie behind the problem and then re-model the strategy or "problem maintaining pattern" so that it no longer occurs.

Sometimes the effort of having to improve their performances is too much for some client's. They feel that it is easier to hang on to their problem than to go through the anticipated effort to change. These client's lack motivation and even though they present themselves as willing client's they will find all kinds of devious ways of getting out of actually having to do something that will actually help them. You have to be very artful with these kinds of client's. You have to be more artful than they are. Usually they are not aware of their patterns of sabotage so direct confrontation is often of no use because they usually go on the defensive if you confront them with your observations.

You can motivate them from the inside by creating a context that will ideally bungee-jump them out of their comfortable position and into action. In these cases it may be beneficial to use imagery techniques to give them an experience of what it would be like to live their lives without their sport.

4. What do you get out of what you're doing now?

When answered consciously, most client's will say that they get nothing out of what they are doing now. However asking client's to identify what they're getting out of what they do now you are also starting to recognise possible secondary gains. Secondary gains are the benefits that client get from having a problem. They often reinforce the problem because they make having the problem more bearable and sometimes even desirable.

5. What could go wrong?

This may seem like a negative question. However, you should recognise, ahead of time, any situations that might stop your client from improving their performance. This question will help you identify the creative ways your client may use to sabotage the intervention process.

A Client-Centered Approach

Obtain a first-person description of the psychological aspects of your client's tournament play.

Then use the following interview questions:

1. Background information about best golfing achievements and experiences.
2. Mental aspects needed to excel in golf.
3. Mental strategies adopted during competition.
4. Information about the preparation for tournament golf.
5. Information about expectations on the golf course.
6. Information about pre-shot routines.
7. Information about internal experiences during optimal performance.
8. Information about reactions to mistakes.
9. Information about beliefs about what they need to do to perform well.

The main aim of this analysis is to explore the experiential knowledge of the player and gain an understanding of the psychological strategies they use during competitions. After gathering this information from the interview, the practitioner should help the player fit their psychological strategies into a preshot routine for putting, driving, iron play, chipping and sand shots. This involves considerable trial and error.

Example case study:

Golfer 1 chose to use a pre-shot routine for iron shots that involved creating a movie of the swing he needed to play the shot. For the driver, the golfer used a pre-shot routine that involved imagining targets on the fairways and focusing attention on the targets during the swing. Before he hit a wedge, sand shot or chip shot, he chose to use a self-talk technique that involved instructing himself on how to play a shot and what he needed to do technically. His putting routine involved imagining the ball roll into the hole before he made his putt. Finally, before each routine the participant used self-talk techniques to create an arousing emotion he described as "exciting" and "confidence". The words and phrases he used were "let's get a birdie", "let's get the ball in the hole", "come on" and, "go for it".

Ideal Performance Qualities

When a golfer successfully puts it all together — both physically and mentally — the resulting performance is exceptional. Those magic moments are termed peak performances.

Mental factors most commonly associated with a peak performance are:

1. feelings of inner calm and being mentally relaxed.
2. feelings of being strong, full of vitality and self-confidence.
3. the absence of worry over the possibility of the lack of control.
4. feelings of uninterrupted concentration.
5. beliefs in one's ability.
6. being absorbed fully in the activity.
7. feelings of control over anxieties, frustrations, emotions, muscle tension and fatigue.
8. feelings of things occurring effortlessly and spontaneously.

The sport literature indicates that golfers need a variety of mental skills to create and maintain a peak performance. Assess your client's mental skills by getting them to complete the questionnaire below:

The Psychological Skills Questionnaire

Rate each question using the following scale:

Strongly Disagree   Strongly Agree

    1   2   3   4   5

Goal Setting

I always set very specific goals before I play.

    1   2   3   4   5

I find it easy to keep to my game plan during competitions.

    1   2   3   4   5

Add up your scores from the statements above. Scores higher than 8 are good; scores lower than 8 mean they need to learn how to set goals and prepare for competitions.

Top tips: Learn how to set goals.

Imaginary Skills

I often imagine how I will feel when I perform in a competition.

    1   2   3   4   5

It is easy for me to form mental pictures.

    1   2   3   4   5

Add up your scores from the statements above. Scores higher than 8 are good; scores lower than 8 mean they need to learn how to use imagery.

Top tips: Use visualization techniques.

Concentration

My concentration never lets me down during important situations.

1   2   3   4   5

I can always concentrate during competitions.

1   2   3   4   5

Add up your scores from the statements above. Scores higher than 8 are good; scores lower than 8 mean they need to learn how to focus.

Top tips: Use a mental pre-shot and post-shot routine.

Self-Talk

I know how to recognise and deal with destructive self-doubt and self-talk.

1   2   3   4   5

I have specific words or phrases that I say to myself to help my performance.

1   2   3   4   5

Add up your scores from the statements above. Scores higher than 8 are good; scores lower than 8 mean they need to change their attitudes.

Top tips: Adopt positive statements or attitudes.

Activating Mental States

I can easily get into the right state of mind before an important competition.

1   2   3   4   5

I know how to control my emotions during competitions.

1   2   3   4   5

Add up your scores from the statements above. Scores higher than 8 are good; scores lower than 8 mean they need to control their emotions.

Top tips: Use imagery, music or focus on positive attitudes in your routines.

Emotions in Sport

30 years of empirical and anecdotal studies strongly indicates that individual success is strongly linked to ones current emotional state. We are now aware any emotion (whether positive toned or negative toned) can have both an optimizing and a dysfunctional effect on performance. Interestingly, emotions deemed to be beneficial to one golfer may prove debilitating for another. Identifying emotional states related to individually successful and poor performances is extremely important if you are to perform at your full potential. The following profile is an individualised assessment programme designed to identify subjective emotional experiences helpful and harmful to your client's performance.

The Optimal Performance Emotion Profile

Get your client to recall their best performances during competitions. Go through the list of emotions below and identify no more than 5 words that describe the helpful positive emotions they felt.

Please think about the intensity of **positive** emotions experienced during best performance. Please rate the intensity from 1 to 10. Where 1 indicates 'nothing at all' and 10 indicates 'extremely strong'.

Helpful positive emotions (P+)

Active, dynamic, energetic, vigorous
Relaxed, comfortable, easy
Calm, peaceful, unhurried, quiet
Cheerful, merry, happy
Confident, certain, sure
Delighted, overjoyed, exhilarated
Determined, set, settled, resolute
Excited, thrilled
Brave, bold, daring, dashing
Glad, pleased, satisfied, contented
Inspired, motivated, stimulated
Light-hearted, carefree,
Nice, pleasant, agreeable
Quick fast, rapid, alert
Place your own emotions here: _____

Now go through the list of emotion below and identify no more than 5 words that describe the helpful negative emotions they felt.

Please think about the intensity of helpful **negative** emotions experienced during best performance. Please rate the intensity from 1 to 10. Where 1 indicates 'nothing at all' and 10 indicates 'extremely strong'.

Helpful negative emotions (N+)

Afraid, fearful, scared, panicky
Angry, aggressive, furious, violent
Annoyed, irritated, distressed
Anxious, apprehensive, worried
Concerned, alarmed, disturbed, dissatisfied
Discouraged, depressed
Doubtful, uncertain, indecisive
Helpless, unsafe, insecure
Inactive, sluggish, lazy
Intense, fierce, jittery, nervous, uneasy
Sorry, unhappy, sad, regretful,
Tense, strained, tight, rigid
Tired, weary, exhausted, worn out
Place your own emotions here: _____

Get your client to recall their worst performances. Go through the list of emotions below and identify no more than 5 words that describe the dysfunctional/harmful positive emotions they felt.

Please think about the intensity of **harmful** positive emotions during your best performance. Please rate the intensity from 1 to 10. Where 1 indicates 'nothing at all' and 10 indicates 'extremely strong'.

Harmful positive emotions (P-)

Active, dynamic, energetic, vigorous
Relaxed, comfortable, easy
Calm, peaceful, unhurried, quiet
Cheerful, merry, happy
Confident, certain, sure
Delighted, overjoyed, exhilarated
Determined, set, settled, resolute
Excited, thrilled
Brave, bold, daring, dashing
Glad, pleased, satisfied, contented
Inspired, motivated, stimulated
Light-hearted, carefree
Nice, pleasant, agreeable
Quick fast, rapid, alert
Place your own emotions here: _____

Now get your client to go through the list of emotion below and identify no more than 5 words that describe the dysfunctional/harmful negative emotions they felt.

Please think about the intensity of **harmful** negative emotions during your best performance. Please rate the intensity from 1 to 10. Where 1 indicates 'nothing at all' and 10 indicates 'extremely strong'.

Harmful negative emotions (N-)

Afraid, fearful, scared, panicky
Angry, aggressive, furious, violent
Annoyed, irritated, distressed, anxious, apprehensive, worried
Concerned, alarmed, disturbed, dissatisfied
Discouraged, depressed
Doubtful, uncertain, indecisive
Helpless, unsafe, insecure
Inactive, sluggish, lazy
Intense, fierce
Jittery, nervous, uneasy
Sorry, unhappy, sad, regretful
Tense, strained, tight, rigid
Tired, weary, exhausted, worn out
Place your own emotions here: _____

See the example profiling chart that follows and then place the emotions your client has identified into the blank profiling chart.

Example Profiling Chart

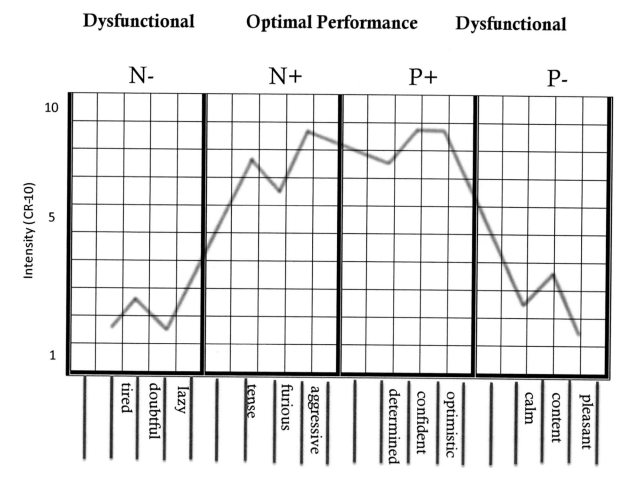

Dysfunctional   **Optimal Performance**   **Dysfunctional**

N-   N+   P+   P-

Intensity (CR-10)

Emotions Experienced

The figure above provides an illustration of an emotion performance profile for a successful golfer. Emotion words selected by this golfer included. For P+ emotions the terms optimistic, confident and determined were used. For N+ emotions the terms aggressive, furious and tense were used. For N- emotions lazy, doubtful and tired were used. For N+ emotions the terms pleasant, calm and relaxed were used. The golfers best performance profile are iceberg-shaped with high intensity scores for (P+ and N+) and lower for the dysfunctional emotions (P- and P+).

The profile of the golfer would suggest optimal performance can be achieved by regulating and controlling emotions termed confidence, optimistic, determination, aggressive, furious and tense.

By working with your client to complete their profile you can predict their own poor and successful performance and set goals to control and regulate the emotions that influence their performances.

Profiling Chart

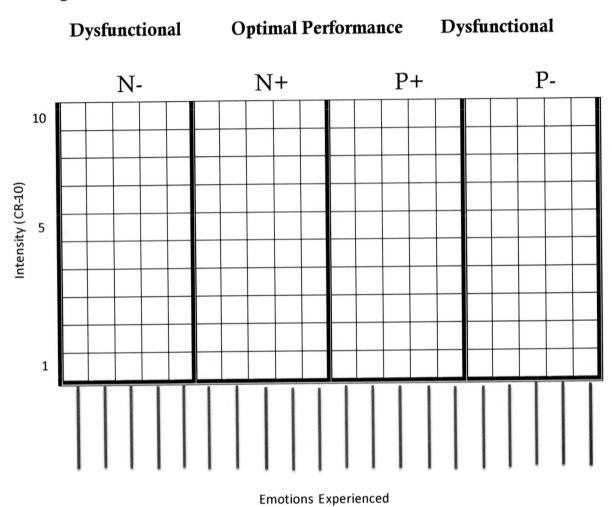

Now you have your client's profile, you need to help them learn how to control emotions. Use the techniques documented in this book.

Positive Emotions

Research in positive psychology and in sports psychology has found a number of positive emotions to be important predictors of a variety of performance and positive healthy behaviors. Optimism for example has been shown to influence both physical and psychological well-being.

Individuals who can regulate positive emotional states differ from negative individuals in several important ways. Most importantly from a performance point of view they approach problems differently and they have the ability to cope with stress and adversity. Specifically, when confronted with a challenge, positive people tend to take a posture of confidence and persistence while negative people are doubtful and hesitant.

Highly successful Olympic champions are characterized by positive emotions, golfers who are unsuccessful do not. Positive emotions that characterize champion golfers are confidence, optimism, happiness determination and hope. Test your client's positive emotional state by asking them to complete the "General Happiness Survey", "The Satisfaction with Life Survey", "The Optimism Survey", "The Confidence Survey" and "The Inspirational Skills Survey".

General Happiness Scale

For each of the following statements and/or questions, please read each one and then click on the dropdown list below it to see the scale. Select the point on the scale that you feel is most appropriate in describing you.

1.   In general I consider myself:

Not a happy person   A happy person

1   2   3   4   5   6   7

2.   Compared to most of my peers, I consider myself:

Less happy   More Happy

1   2   3   4   5   6   7

3.   Some people are generally very happy. They enjoy life regardless of what is going on, getting the most out of everything. To what extent does this characterization describe you?

Not at all   A great deal

1   2   3   4   5   6   7

4.   Some people are generally not very happy. Although they are not depressed, they never seem as happy as they might be. To what extent does this characterization describe you?

A great deal   Not at all

1   2   3   4   5   6   7

A score greater than 24 means you are very happy. A score lower than 16 means you need to work on making yourself happy.

Top tips: Write down all of the things that make you happy and set a goal to do at least one of those things every day.

Satisfaction with Life Scale

Below are five statements that you may agree or disagree with. Read each one and then select the response that best describes how strongly you agree or disagree.

Strongly disagree   Strongly agree

1   2   3   4   5   6   7

1.   In most ways, my life is close to my ideal.

    1   2   3   4   5   6   7

2.   The conditions of my life are excellent.

    1   2   3   4   5   6   7

3.   I am completely satisfied with my life.

    1   2   3   4   5   6   7

4.   So far I have gotten the most important things I want in life.

    1   2   3   4   5   6   7

5.   If I could live my life over, I would change nothing.

    1   2   3   4   5   6   7

A score greater than 25 means you are generally satisfied with your life. A score lower than 20 means you need to work on enhancing your satisfaction with life.

Top tips: Write down all of the things that would satisfy you and set a goal to achieve this target.

The Optimism Survey

Below are three statements about how optimistic you are. Read each statement and select how much the statement is like you. Please be honest and accurate! Use the following scale to answer the questions.

Not like me		somewhat like me		very much like me
1	2	3	4	5

1.   I often think great things will happen to me.

       1   2   3   4   5

2.   I often think about things that inspire me.

       1   2   3   4   5

3.   I am always in an optimistic mood.

       1   2   3   4   5

A score greater than 12 means you are very optimistic. A score lower than 9 means you need to work on developing your optimistic attitude.

Top tips: You can be more optimistic by writing down all of the great things that could happen to you and setting courageous goals.

The Power of Confidence

Research on golfers indicates that the major predictor of flow or peak performance is confidence. Self-confidence is defined as a belief about your capabilities to produce a certain level of performance. Confident beliefs determine how you feel, think, motivate yourself, and behave.

For example, confident golfers approach difficult tasks as challenges to be mastered rather than as threats to be avoided. This outlook fosters intrinsic interest and deep engrossment in practicing to master certain skills.

Confident people also set themselves challenging goals and maintain a strong commitment to them. They also heighten and sustain their efforts in the face of failure and they attribute failure to insufficient effort or deficient knowledge and skills that are acquirable. Such an efficacious outlook produces personal accomplishments, reduces stress, and creates great players.

Sources of Confidence

People's beliefs about their confidence can be developed by four main sources of influence.

1. Performance accomplishments
2. Vicarious experience
3. Verbal persuasion
4. Emotional arousal

Performance Accomplishments

The most effective way of creating a strong sense of confidence is through mastery experiences. Successes build a robust belief in your personal confidence. Failures undermine it, especially if failures occur before a sense of confidence is firmly established.

The best way of achieving success is to set achievable goals that help you master certain skills. It is important you structure situations that bring success and avoid placing yourself in situations where you are likely to fail. The goal setting section will help you develop this behaviour more effectively. When using the goal setting skills section, try to measure success in terms of self-improvement rather than by triumphs over others.

Vicarious Experiences

The second way of creating and strengthening beliefs about confidence is through the vicarious experiences provided by role models. Seeing people similar to yourself succeed by sustained effort raises your belief that you too possess the capabilities to master the skills needed to achieve peak performance.

Competent role models transmit knowledge and teach you effective skills and strategies.

The best ways of obtaining positive vicarious experiences is to watch highly skilled people perform. Even the greatest players in the world have role models; in the golfing world Tiger Woods had Jack Nicklaus, and Jack Nicklaus had Bobby Jones. Who ever you choose as your role models, watch them in action, if possible read their autobiography or watch them on YouTube, during their most influential and inspirational moments. We learn so much through imitating successful models, so spend time each day watching and learning their skills.

Verbal Persuasion

Social persuasion is a third way of strengthening people's beliefs. Players who are given praise are more likely to mobilise greater effort.

A good coach will always give positive comments; however, you can help yourself by positive self-talk. See the section on self-talk to give yourself more help in this area.

It is also important that you build a team around you that gives you great advice and provides you with a positive environment. All of the best golfers and performance people have an entourage of people that coach them and provide a supportive positive climate.

However, it is worth noting here the team members must evaluate have constructive debates and challenge. This will avoid group think. It is important to remember a completely cohesive team is likely to have blind spots.

Emotional Arousal

Successful confidence builders do more than say positive things. People also rely partly on their emotional states in judging their capabilities. Positive moods enhance perceived confidence, and despondent moods diminish it. Mood also affects people's judgments and the ability to make good decisions.

It is not the sheer intensity of emotional and physical reactions that is important, but rather how they are perceived and interpreted. Great golfers and performance people view their state of affective arousal as an energising facilitator of performance, whereas those who are beset by self-doubts regard their arousal as debilitating. Indeed, great golfers often state when they are in contention to win they feel excitement.

The Self-Confidence Survey

Test you level of confidence by completing the survey below. When you have finished this test you can improve your confidence by using the mental skills development strategies described in later sections.

Rate each question using the following scale:

Strongly Disagree   Strongly Agree

        1   2   3   4   5

Please answer the following in relation to your experience. There are no right or wrong answers. Circle the number that best matches your experience.

1.   I usually think I'm a good at the job I do

        1   2   3   4   5

2.   I will not be satisfied until I am the best.

        1   2   3   4   5

3.   When I am faced with a difficult situation, I'm usually sure I will be able to handle it.

        1   2   3   4   5

4.   I'm very confident about my ability.

        1   2   3   4   5

5.   I often think about my best experiences when I go to into competitions.

        1   2   3   4   5

6.   I am always in a good positive mood.

        1   2   3   4   5

7.   I always tell myself positive things.

        1   2   3   4   5

8.   I often think about things at that inspire me.

        1   2   3   4   5

9.   I often tell myself I can become great at my chosen profession.

     1   2   3   4   5

10.   I often think about achieving great things.

     1   2   3   4   5

A score greater than 40 means you are very self-confident A score lower than 30 means you need to work on developing your self-confidence.

Top tips: You can improve your confidence by setting process and courageous goals. Go to the section on goal setting.

The Power of Inspiration

Inspiration is an emotional state that produces high levels of drive and motivates all of us to want to achieve great things. Inspiration is the key to peak performance and is fundamental to positive emotional development, emotional regulation and knowledge creation. Other positive emotions such as passion, optimism and hope are forged from inspirational thoughts.

"A person's results are a direct result of their levels of aspiration and inspiration."

- Jack Nicklaus -

Players who are inspirational are idea catalysts, energetic, tenacious and above all passionate about what they do. They are people who create a vision framework for them to follow. They are friendly, supportive, fun loving and above all have the skills to develop strong relationships and evoke positive emotions in others. The difference between winning and losing can be attributed to their power to arouse positive emotions through their inspirational thinking and performances.

Positive emotions have an impact on our thoughts and decision-making processes. Inspirational people are shielded from negative emotions they set courageous goals and create opportunities that help them achieve greatness. They are people that empower other people and set our spirits free. It is their ability to inspire themselves rather than their personality that sustain their success.

The Inspirational Skills Survey

Rate each question using the following scale:

Strongly Disagree   Strongly Agree

     1   2   3   4   5

1.   You have lots of inspirational ideas?

     1   2   3   4   5

2.   You enjoy creating new ways of working and thinking?

     1   2   3   4   5

3.   You recognize your strengths and you focus on them?

     1   2   3   4   5

4.   You support other players in achieving their goals?

     1   2   3   4   5

5.   Your open to new ideas?

     1   2   3   4   5

6.   You are ambitious about your future?

     1   2   3   4   5

7.   Are you energetic in training?

     1   2   3   4   5

8.   You spare time to speak to everybody?

     1   2   3   4   5

9.   You are confident?

     1   2   3   4   5

10.   You are a reflective thinker?

     1   2   3   4   5

11. You constantly seek making improvements to your game?

   1   2   3   4   5

12. You are jovial and fun loving?

   1   2   3   4   5

13. You are committed to achieving great things?

   1   2   3   4   5

14. You are passionate about playing?

   1   2   3   4   5

15. You are tenacious and uncompromising about achieving success?

   1   2   3   4   5

16. You have high levels of determination?

   1   2   3   4   5

17. You a networker and alliance builder?

   1   2   3   4   5

18. You are friendly to everyone during competitions?

   1   2   3   4   5

19. You are generous to your colleagues?

   1   2   3   4   5

20. You are a good problem solver?

   1   2   3   4   5

21. You are unshakable at achieving your dreams?

   1   2   3   4   5

22. You have the will to achieve success?

   1   2   3   4   5

23. You are trusted by your colleagues?

    1   2   3   4   5

24. You are people oriented?

    1   2   3   4   5

25. You stay focused on your ideas?

    1   2   3   4   5

Add up your scores from the questions above. Scores higher than 80 show you are an inspirational person. Scores lower mean that you need build your inspirational skills. The table below is designed to help you identify the skills of an inspirational thinker.

Top tips: Watch movies or you-tube clips of events and people who inspire you. Watching Jack Nicklaus win the 1986 masters would be a good start.

The Skills of an Inspirational Player

Self-awareness	Self-regulation	Motivation	Empathy	Social Skills
Comprehend the big picture	Idea catalyst	Motivates	Inspirational	Problem solver
Reflective thinker	Inventor	Emotional	Outgoing	Consummate communicator
Personal responsibility	Open to new ideas	People catalyst	People orientated	Poise and grace
Fearsome intellect	Seek improvement	Mobilise people	Time for everybody	Avuncular and jovial
Mighty figure	Challenging	Coaching	Gets the best from people	Fun loving
	Push the envelope	Supportive	Networker and alliance builder	Friendly
	Watches and observes	Involved in all activities	Praises and rewards	Flair and flexibility
	Hardworking	Coaxing and influencing	Provide purpose to staff	Strong and clear thinker
	Energetic	Revered for knowledge	Supporter of employees	Focused
	Ambitious	Love of the industry	Shares the dream	Foresight
	Grit and determination	Lifetime involvement	Designer and keeper of the dream	
	Unrelenting, uncompromising commitment	Stability and direction	Sustain and energise the dream	
	Unshakeable			
	Tenacious			
	Determination			
	Energetic			
	Dynamic			
	Passionate			
	Passion for work			
	Passion for a challenge			

Peak Performance

Peak performance occurs when golfers stop 'conscious processing' (analysing their technique or the consequences of their behaviour during their performance). When golfers achieve this they experience a holistic sensation of absorption and they act with total involvement. This mental state is called 'the zone' or 'flow'.

Neurological research evidence suggests when a peak performance occurs the functions of the right hemisphere of the brain become activated and the corresponding functions of the left hemisphere of the brain become deactivated. The shift in consciousness from the left hemisphere (logical and analytical mode) to the right hemisphere (creative and intuitive) is thought to give better access to the functions of the brain which are important for good athletic performance. The diagram below shows the functions of the cerebral hemispheres more clearly.

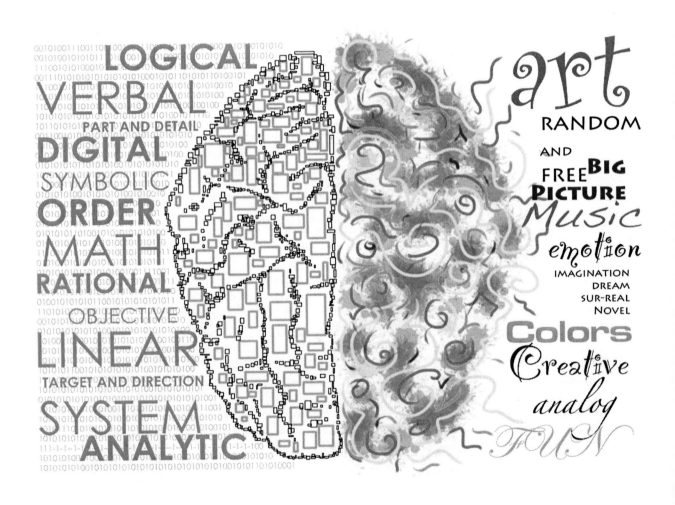

The Wheel of Peak Performance

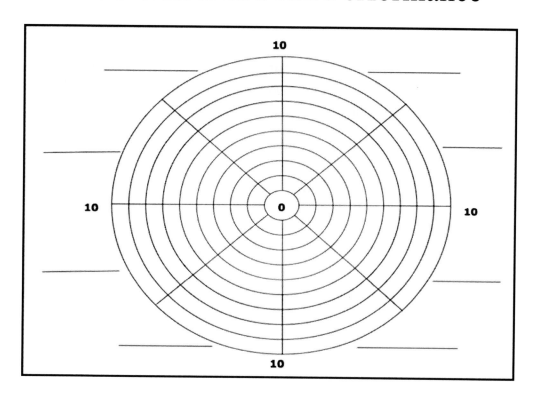

The characteristics of flow are:

- The feeling that performance is effortless
- Clear goals
- Total concentration on task
- Complete control without consciously doing so
- No self-consciousness or evaluation
- Time transformation it is perceived as either speeding u or slowing down
- An autotelic experience.

Rate your current perceptions of peak performance during competitions from 1-10. A score of 1 is very low and score of 10 is very high.

Once you have completed this profile you will realize you have areas of certain strengths and weaknesses. The wheel will tell you what you need to work on in the future.

Top tips: Use imagery and music to control flow.

Mental Toughness

For many years the term mental toughness has been associated with sporting excellence and highlighted as an important psychological contributor to successful performance. Mental toughness is all about having a psychological edge that enables you to consistently remain determined, focused, confident, and in control under competitive pressure.

Researchers have shown that the main attributes of a mentally tough individual are as follows:

- A belief in your ability to achieve success (i.e. **self-belief**).

- The ability to focus on what is relevant while minimizing irrelevant information (i.e. **attention control**).

- The ability to persevere through difficult times and bounce back from setbacks (i.e. **resilience**).

- The desire for achieving success and acting upon such thoughts (i.e. **successful mindset**).

- The tendency to expect positive outcomes in the future, and to view oneself in a positive manner (i.e. **optimistic thinking**).

- An awareness of and ability to use emotions to facilitate optimal outcomes (i.e. **emotional awareness and regulation**).

- Thriving when challenged to execute the required skills and procedures effectively (i.e. **handle challenge**).

- An awareness and understanding of the performance environment and how to apply this knowledge to achieve success (i.e. **context intelligence**).

The Wheel of Mental Toughness

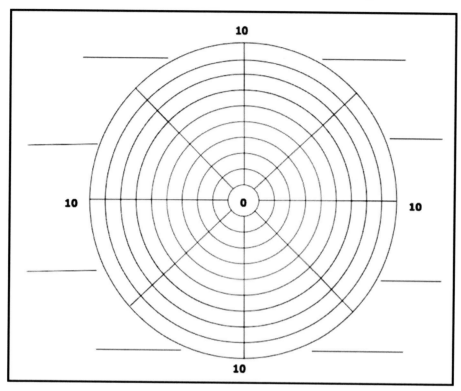

- Successful mindset – desire to achieve success
- Resilience – ability to persevere through adversity and bounce back after set backs
- Self-belief
- Optimistic
- Attention control – ability to focus
- Emotional control and regulation
- Thrive when challenged
- Context intelligence

Rate your current perceptions of your self from 1-10. A score of 1 is very low and score of 10 is very high.

Once you have completed this profile you will realize you have areas of certain strengths and weaknesses. The wheel will tell you what you need to work on in the future.

Top tips: Set a goal to improve one of the main attributes of mental toughness.

The Successful Mindset Survey

Below are 16 statements about your mindset. Read each statement and select how much the statement is like you. Please be honest and accurate! Use the following scale to answer the questions.

Not like me   somewhat like me   very much like me

1   2   3   4   5

1.   I aim to be the best in the world at what I do

1   2   3   4   5

2.   I often set a goal but later choose to pursue a different one

1   2   3   4   5

3.   I am diligent

1   2   3   4   5

4.   Failures double my motivation to succeed.

1   2   3   4   5

5.   I am ambitious.

1   2   3   4   5

6.   My interests are consistent from year to year.

1   2   3   4   5

7.   I am persistent.

1   2   3   4   5

8.   I become interested in new pursuits every few months.

1   2   3   4   5

9.   I finish whatever I begin.

1   2   3   4   5

10. New ideas and new projects sometimes distract me from old ones.

   1   2   3   4   5

11. I am a hard worker.

   1   2   3   4   5

12. Achieving something of lasting importance is the highest goal in life.

   1   2   3   4   5

13. Setbacks don't discourage me.

   1   2   3   4   5

14. I am driven to succeed.

   1   2   3   4   5

15. I have overcome setbacks to conquer an important challenge.

   1   2   3   4   5

16. I have achieved a goal that took years of work.

   1   2   3   4   5

Add up your scores from the questions above. If you score more than 50 you have a strong mindset. If you score below 50 work on developing a positive attitude.

Top tips: Go to the 'Positive Attitudes for Golfers' section.

Strength-Based Approach

Thirty years of research have found that the most successful golfers are those who believe they get to do what they do best every day. Research also tells us that if you focus on your human strengths (rather than the absence of human weaknesses) you can improve performance. Strength based approaches also act as buffers against mental illness.

The Strengths Test

What are your client's strengths? Below is a list of common human and golf strengths. From the list, ask your client to circle the strengths that best describes them.

Great Putter   Great driver

Great Iron player   Great pitcher

Great at sand saves   Ingenuity

Creativity   Desire to achieve success

Audacious   Optimistic

Keeping focused   Controlling my emotions

Resilient   Able to Set Goals

Able to visualise   Able to focus attention

Able to use self-talk   Enthusiastic

Confident   Self-belief

Love of learning   Able to have fun

Brave   Courageous

Hard working   Industrious

Energy   Enthusiastic

Optimistic   Playful

Humour   Appreciation of excellence

Fairness

Add any other strengths here: _____

Now you have an awareness of your strengths and what you are best at, answer the following questions using the following scale:

Strongly disagree   Strongly agree

    1   2   3   4   5

1.   Do you practice what you are best at every day?

    1   2   3   4   5

2.   Are you doing something you are really passionate about?

    1   2   3   4   5

A score greater than 8 means you are working to your strengths everyday and so likely to feel motivated and a achieve your goals. Scores below 8 suggest you are not working to your strengths and maybe feeling frustrated at competitions and not performing to your best.

Top tips: Set a goal to practice your strengths every day.

Attitudes and Beliefs

Our brains are wired for beliefs, and when activated, the body responds as if the belief is reality, producing our results. Our brains cannot distinguish external from internal 'reality.' So if inside we believe we cannot do something, we will struggle every time we attempt it. The only way we can change the results we get is by changing that belief.

People create their own realities of the world. We create our own reality by using filters to distort, delete, and generalize information that we receive. We have all had different experiences which have created our own set of filters, which comprise of our values, memories, attitudes, and beliefs. That's why everyone has his or her own opinion and view on things. By changing our beliefs inside ourselves, we can create a new reality and, in turn, have a massive effect on what we are capable of.

An example here would be if you held a deep belief that you were always unlucky when you played golf. You would delete all experiences of when you got fortunate breaks. Instead, you would highlight only your bad breaks to yourself and others, and your belief would continue to hold true and be your 'reality.'

Often, a golfer's limiting belief only activates under certain circumstances, leading to a negative result under pressure. That is why players often get the same results at critical moments (a crucial putt on the 18th green, a drive on a certain hole, or a game against a certain opponent).

When a limiting belief is activated, it leads to a negative effect on our states and physiology, often demonstrated by anxiety and tension in the body. Finding these beliefs and helping players to change them will have a dramatic effect on their results.

An example of the power of beliefs:

Before Sir Roger Bannister broke the 4 minute mile in 1954, medical experts believed that it was medically unsafe for anyone to achieve it. Consequently, no runners believed they could do it. Once the barrier had been broken, someone had conquered the impossible. Within a year of Bannister's record, 37 more runners broke the 4 minute barrier. A year later another 300 broke it.

The powerful magic that made it possible was simply a change in BELIEF.

In the above example, runners did not suddenly become magically fitter or faster. They had not taken any new fitness or strength training that allowed them to break the 4 minute mile. Instead, the change in their beliefs had led to a change in their own states and physiology, which in turn led to them reaching a new level of performance.

Beliefs can be about yourself, about others, about your abilities, and about external factors.

It has been said that we can't outperform our own self-image. These are beliefs we have about ourselves as people.

Examples:
>   I don't deserve/am not worthy to succeed.
>   I'm bad/stupid/lazy.
>   If I succeed, then people won't like/love/want me.
>   I'm not a lucky person.

Some people are not consciously aware that they have this type of belief; they just carry it around like a piece of excess luggage. Because it's been there so long, they assume something like 'that's the way I am,' without questioning it. You may be aware of an inner voice, which just nags away with jibes such as:

>   'You're not good enough.'
>   'You don't deserve to be here.'

Often our own beliefs about what we are capable of severely limit us. By pushing our boundaries of what we believe we are capable of, we can aspire to new levels.

Annika Sorenstam believed that she could shoot 54 every time she went out to play. This was part of her VISION54 that was invented by her own psychologist. To believe that we can shoot 54 for eighteen holes is a brilliant shift in the world view, overriding the belief that par is perfection and that every green requires two putts. Shortly after she made this paradigm shift, Annika shot a 59.

We can also have beliefs about other people and outside factors such as these:

> Life's purely a game of chance.
> I need better resources to perform well.
> I can't play in these conditions.

We must accept that we are responsible for everything that happens to us and that nothing else can take any blame.

Make a list of 5 situations where, for some reason, you did not perform well when it mattered.

1)

2)

3)

4)

5)

Write down the beliefs you have about that situation in the limiting belief column.

Situation	Limiting Belief
1)	
2)	
3)	
4)	
5)	

Now write down the impact it would make to your game if you no longer had these beliefs.

Limiting Belief	Result of Change in Belief
1)	
2)	
3)	
4)	
5)	

Remember beliefs are not truths. Challenge your beliefs and change them to more positive ones.

Attitudes

An attitude is "a relatively enduring organization of beliefs, feelings, and behavioral tendencies towards socially significant objects, groups, events or symbols".

Structure of Attitudes

Attitudes structure can be described in terms of **three components**.

1. **Affective** component: this involves a person's feelings / emotions about the attitude object. For example: "I am scared of spiders".

2. **Behavioral** (or conative) component: the way the attitude we have influences how we act or behave. For example: "I will avoid spiders and scream if I see one".

3. **Cognitive** component: this involves a person's belief / knowledge about an attitude object. For example: "I believe spiders are dangerous".

This model is known as the **ABC model of attitudes**. The three components are usually linked. However, there is evidence that the cognitive and affective components of behavior do not always match with behavior.

The Function of Attitudes

Attitudes can serve several functions for the individual.

Knowledge. Attitudes provide meaning (knowledge) for life. The knowledge function refers to our need for a world that is consistent and relatively stable. This allows us to **predict** what is likely to happen, and so gives us a sense of control. Attitudes can help us organize and structure our experience. Knowing a person's attitude helps us predict their behavior. For example, knowing that a person is a poor putter we can predict they will consistently miss putts.

Self / Ego-expressive. The attitudes we express (1) help **communicate** who we are and (2) may make us feel good because we have asserted our identity. Self-expression of attitudes can be non-verbal too: think bumper sticker, cap, or T-shirt slogan. Therefore, our attitudes are part of our identify, and help us to be aware through expression of our feelings, beliefs and values.

Adaptive. If a person holds and/or expresses socially acceptable attitudes, other people will reward them with approval and **social acceptance**. For example, when people flatter their bosses or instructors (and believe it) or keep silent if they think an attitude is unpopular. Again, expression can be nonverbal [think politician kissing baby]. Attitudes then, are to do with being apart of a social group and the adaptive functions helps us fit in with a social group. People seek out others who share their attitudes, and develop similar attitudes to those they like.

The **ego-defensive** function refers to holding attitudes that **protect** our self-esteem or that justify actions that make us feel guilty. For example, one way children might defend themselves against the feelings of humiliation they have experienced in P.E. lessons is to adopt a strongly negative attitude to all sport. People whose pride has suffered following a defeat in sport might similarly adopt a defensive attitude: "I'm not bothered, I'm sick of rugby anyway…". This function has psychiatric overtones. Positive attitudes towards ourselves, for example, have a protective function (i.e. an ego-defensive role) in helping us preserve our self-image.

The basic idea behind the functional approach is that attitudes help a person to mediate between their own inner needs (expression, defense) and the outside world (adaptive and knowledge).

Below are some attitudes that may help you overcome your own boundaries.

"Work like you don't need the money

Love like you've never been hurt

Dance like nobody's watching

Sing like nobody's listening

Live like it's heaven on earth"

- attributed to William Purkey -

Attitude Advice from the Greats

Tiger Woods:

"The biggest thing is to have the mind-set and the belief you can win every tournament going on. A lot of guys don't have that; Nicklaus had it. He felt he was going to beat everybody".

"No matter how good you get you can always get better and that's the exciting part".

"I'm trying as hard as I can, and sometimes things don't go your way, and that's the way things go".

"I've busted my butt on the range for hours on end and made changes to get to this point where I'm able to compete at the highest level in major championships. That's where you want to be".

"I don't hit every green I don't birdie every hole I don't win every tournament but I believe I will".

Seve Ballesteros:

"I look into their eyes, shake their hand, pat their back, and wish them luck, but I am thinking, 'I am going to bury you'".

"I know where I am and I know which way I'm going, ... Only winning will satisfy me. You don't think it is possible? It is very possible".

Jack Nicklaus:

"'I don't give a darn' attitude is probably why I've shot so many good final rounds over the years when I started the day a few shots behind with nothing to lose. . .".

"I never hit a shot, not even in practice, without having a very sharp, in-focus picture of it in my head".

Bobby Jones:

"The secret of golf is to turn three shots into two".

"In order to win, you must play your best golf when you need it most, and play your sloppy stuff when you can afford it".

"It is nevertheless a game of considerable passion, either of the explosive type, or that which burns inwardly and sears the soul".

"I never learned anything from a match that I won".

Ben Hogan:

"The most important shot in golf is the next one".

"I dreamed one night that I had 17 holes-in-one and one two, and when I woke up I was so god dam mad".

Lee Trevino:

"I'm a golfaholic, no question about that. Counseling wouldn't help me. They'd have to put me in prison, and then I'd talk the warden into building a hole or two and teach him how to play".

Arnold Palmer:

"What other people may find in poetry or art museums, I find in the flight of a good drive".

Positive Attitudes for Golfers

I am going to try to win every tournament

I am going to try to hole every shot

I am going to try to hole every putt

Always think about winning

I am going to be the best out here

Goal Setting

"The man who moved the mountain was the one that took away the small stones first"

- Confucius -

After each session it is important for you to set your client's some goals. Goal setting can enhance performance in several ways, **provided that the goals are accepted as being realistic and worthwhile** goals will help you to:

- Maintain effort and persistence in the face of setbacks and temporary failures.
- Find new strategies to achieve the goal.
- Develop self-confidence and positive attitudes by experiencing success and goal achievement.

Types of Goals

Product/Outcome Goals

Outcome goals are goals that focus on results and consequences. A good example would be becoming the world's leader at what you do. It is extremely important to realize that while outcome goals are important motivators, at best you only have partial control over them. For this reason, it is suggested that short and mid-term goals should be performance or process/experience orientated. Product or outcome orientated goals generally exert a strong motivational influence. Consequently, they usually are very effective for intermediate or long-term aims or when effort (rather than skill) is the crucial variable.

Experience/Process Goals

Goals that are experience orientated focus on the client's mindset and mental state. For example, doing what you do best everyday. Goals that are process orientated will focus on HOW you will achieve an outcome goal and usually directs attention to performing a skill or experiencing a certain mental state. Furthermore, process orientated goals can also directly help you to:

1. Give you a mind-set ready to perform.
2. Direct attention towards priority sources of information (i.e. concentrate).
3. Proportionately allocate sufficient effort to priority aspects of the task.

Furthermore, process goals are more flexible than outcome goals in other words they can easily be changed to satisfy the immediate needs of the client. Process orientated goals usually exert a stronger influence when skill is a crucial variable.

Performance Goals

Goals that are performance orientated (e.g. achieving production targets). They direct your focus on future improvements relative to past performance. Performance and process/experience goals are in your control and this feature helps develop confidence and improved performance.

Courageous Goals

These are goals that inspire and challenge people (e.g. finding a cure for cancer). They activate you to behave with boldness and courage. In golf it may involve breaking away from processes, systems and rules and it often means setting goals that are seen by many as impossible. It involves questioning traditional orthodoxy and leads us in to developing new ideas and innovations.

How to help your client plan and structure a set of goals

Below shows an example of multiple goals for a player about to start a course of mental training to improve his 'emotional control in competitions.

Long term aim	Goals for next month	Goals and courses of action for this week
	1) Learn how to set goals	1.1 Set aside a fixed time to practice goal setting each day. 1.2 Write down negative thoughts each day. Pick out the worst one and use goal-setting to transform it into a positive statement 1.3 Construct my own set of goals for next week
A. Acquire mental skills to improve performance	2) Learn how to control anxiety before a competition. 3) Learn how to use mental rehearsal	2.1 Find out if there is anyone whom I could discuss controlling my nerves. 2.2 Develop a mental training programme to help me cope.
B. Improve performance	4) Improve my ability to control anger.	4.1 Thirty minutes of mental rehearsal on how I could react better to things that anger me.
C. Achieve my dream		

Use this Goal Setting chart for your own clients.

Long term aim	Goals for next month	Goals and courses of action for this week
	1)	1.1 1.2 1.3
A.	2)	2.1 2.2
B.	3)	3.1
C.		

A Case Study

Professional golfers who are playing badly do not make good company. They are to be avoided. Conversation with struggling players may start innocently on a general topic of conversation such as soccer or the fuel economy of the Ford Mondeo, but the subject matter quickly returns to missed cuts and blocked drives.

Other Tour players, unless they are close friends, make a point of keeping out of their way, as if mediocre performances are infectious, a rare and unpleasant virus that could be picked up in the same way you catch a cold.

Players in a slump find it difficult to manufacture confidence. They believe that feeling good about their game is a long process that can take days or weeks or even months. The professional golfer who is susceptible to negative self-analysis, sees confidence through the eyes of a competent builder erecting a house without assistance.

And every time he conducts a satisfactory session on the range or successfully holes a difficult putt, in his mind they are individual bricks laid skilfully, small but important steps on the way to completing his house of confidence.

After a while he'll risk telling anyone who'll listen that he's 'hitting the ball well' or that 'I'm really popping my new driver'. And for a short time, usually no longer than a few days, he'll find he's 'in the zone' and shooting low. Then it all goes wrong. His house of confidence is blown away by a theoretical hurricane and he's left sifting through the rubble searching for an answer, and a quick way to 'get back in the zone', his confidence evaporated in an instant like sticking a pin in a balloon. Pop! And he's back at the range blasting balls and looking despairingly for a technical solution.

Scottish international Stephen Gallacher was in a slump when he arrived at the Italian Open at Olgiata Golf Club, just outside Rome. He had survived just two cuts from his previous 11 tournaments and finished 103rd, 101st and joint 106th in three of his last four events. Golf journalists found it impossible to prevent themselves from referring to his form as 'disappointing' and he was developing a nagging reputation for unfulfilled potential.

Stephen turned professional in 1994 when his handicap was plus four, which means he was so good he had to add four shots to his final total. He enjoyed an amateur career you would die for. Stephen played off scratch when he was 16 and won dozens of tournaments including the Scottish Boys Championships (twice), the Scottish Amateur, the Scottish Youths, the European Championship and the Lytham Trophy. But now, after nine years with the big boys, he had not won a tournament and self-doubt had begun to erode his ability.

"When I was an amateur, I was winning everything," says Stephen. "Whenever I turned up, I expected to win. In fact, I knew I was going to win, even when I wasn't playing well. I had to get back into that frame of mind as a pro but I didn't know where to start. Then I met sports psychologist John Pates and my whole life changed.

"I'd seen this big guy around the Tour and, to be honest, I thought he was a rep for Titleist. My pal Gary Emerson had introduced us the week before the Italian Open in Rome. I told John I was struggling and that I needed to sort out my mind but I hadn't seen the right person.

"I hadn't played well for two months. I was trying too hard and getting in my own way, forcing everything and getting nervous. We chatted for 15 minutes on the putting green and I liked what he was saying. It was all so simple and made such good sense."

John and Stephen had talked briefly several times over the previous few days, often just for a few minutes. The total amount of time they had spent together did not exceed one hour but it had provided information that enabled John to identify the areas Stephen had to work on to improve his form.

Firstly, and most importantly, he had developed an irrational faith in technique so that he was unable to hit a ball without the comfort of concentrating on positions and swing thoughts, which just happened to be the opposite of what he should be doing - freeing his mind.

No matter how hard Stephen tried to eradicate negative thoughts when he was not playing well, they would return without warning, nibbling away at the edges of his mind, reminding him of that three-foot putt he missed the week before or the blocked drive that careered out of bounds.

Stephen had also found it difficult to 'get in the zone' - a positive state of mind he found so effortlessly as a young amateur. Finally, his pre-shot routine had become unpredictable and erratic.

"I admit I was very technically minded," says Stephen. "As an amateur, I just went for all my shots. I'd hole more putts because I wasn't worried about my stroke - I just picked the line and whacked it. But when I turned pro I started to think about the line and read too much into it. I was steering the ball and I had become scared in case I missed.

"Bob Torrance was my coach back then and he was really good at motivating. He would say to me, 'You're the best and you're ready' - you know, stuff like that.

"A guy called John Mathers came to help the Scottish squad about 10 years ago but a lot of the players laughed at him because none of us had done anything like that before.

"As for when I played in the Walker Cup, well, there was no psychology at all. We all thought it was a backward step. We just played - that was it. For me it was all about swinging well and hitting the ball. If I was hitting my driver well, then I would play well. It went right through my game.

"I knew I had to get that feeling back but I didn't know how."

The two men had much to talk about. Back in Madrid, they had made an agreement to work together, at some unspecified time in the future. This meeting on the putting green in Italy had been unplanned, but Stephen was determined to make the most of it.

"I'm going to hit a few balls on the range before I tee off. Will you come with me, John?" he asked.

Stephen loosened up and began hitting nine irons with purpose, timing his shots adequately but not perfectly and certainly not to the preposterously high standards of a European Tour player who has won more than £600,000.

"What are you thinking about before you play a shot?" asked John.

"Well, actually, I'm trying to make sure my club is just a touch outside the line on the backswing," Stephen said, with a sense of accomplishment.

"Oh, yes," said John, sternly.

Stephen continued: "That's something I'm working on with my coach at the moment." "Tell me," said John. "When was the last really good shot you hit under pressure? When were you last in the zone?"

It was an easy answer. The week before, in Madrid, Stephen had just six holes of the second round to play and he was one shot inside the cut. All he had to do was par in and he knew he would be playing at the weekend, a considerable accomplishment considering his recent form. Then he had a six, two-over-par, the result of a clumsy mistake, so he needed to birdie two of the last four holes or he would be packing his suitcase early - an unpleasant task he had become familiar with.

"I needed to make the cut in Spain to keep my card," Stephen said. "After that double bogey, I had to make two birdies, which made me angry and got me up a bit. On the next hole I hit it to four feet for an eagle and although I missed the putt, I wasn't worried.

"Then I just missed the green on the 17th. I looked at the shot and somehow I just knew I was going to hole it. I looked at my caddy and said: 'This is going in.' I took out my lob wedge and that was it - in it went. I've always been able to do that when I really needed to."

John smiled and said: "Don't you think it would be better to play in that frame of mind all the time instead of thinking about technique? You can. Just concentrate. Get an image in your mind of holing that chip and how you felt. Recall all those good feelings."

So Stephen closed his eyes and returned to the 17th green at Madrid. He recalled the striped shirt his caddie was wearing and the statistical information of the hole in question, which was a 374-yard par four, dogleg to the right.

He saw his wedge approach shot, which he pushed slightly, just a hint but enough for the ball to drift to the right, missing the green by no more than a yard, perhaps 20 feet from the hole.

Stephen is alongside his caddy now, with a lob wedge in his hand, crouching down, concentrating, seeing the line perfectly and the ball's moving along the green on its predetermined path towards the hole, as if it is being sucked in by an invisible force. In it went, his caddy thumps his fist in the air, the memory real, the sensation so powerful a smile of satisfaction works its way across his face.

He felt good. Confident. Invincible. "Now hit a shot," said John.

So he did. And the ball soared in the air, straight as an arrow, landing softly alongside the pin fluttering softly in the distance 130 yards away, backspin zipping it back gently a few feet. Stephen went through the same routine again and again, each time moving in his mind back to Madrid and returning to the present in an instant, positive thoughts flooding through his brain.

He changed clubs several times but the result was always the same, an effortless swing he did not think about, the ball flying obediently to the target. He had an image of being inside a mechanical robot on a car assembly line, completing a complicated task efficiently, over and over again.

A tentative smile of appreciation spread across his face and Stephen announced boldly: "Right, I'm going to use this today, on the course. I'm ready." The two men shook hands warmly, the teacher and pupil, celebrating a job well done.

Stephen headed towards the first tee, where a large crowd awaited him, non-golfers mainly, dark-skinned Italians puffing cigarettes, drinking cans of Coca-Cola and looking cool in their designer sun glasses.

He had a spring in his step, an excitement he had not felt for some time. Stephen now believed he could get in the zone whenever it was necessary and that confidence was a natural force of energy he could tap into at will, like plugging in an electric kettle.

Brian Davies and Robert Karlsson, his partners for the first round, were waiting for him. Stephen was not familiar with such positive thoughts. The first tee can be a daunting place for a professional golfer without confidence. He is aware of the crowd, the pressure and the indignities a difficult course can subject him to. But not today.

The first hole at Olgiata is a tight par-four of 378 yards with a narrow fairway the width of a country road and a green smaller than the average living room, surrounded by bunkers. Stephen's name was announced to the crowd, who stopped talking instantly, the silence eerie and unsettling.

He pulled out his driver, took a short mental trip back to his chip-in at Madrid, focused on the ball, then the target and away it went, his cocoon of concentration broken by the applause of the crowd, clapping enthusiastically, a hint of awe in their actions as the ball exploded into the distance, splitting the fairway more than 300 yards away.

That drive was the first step in the reconstruction of his career. He went on to shoot 69, three under par, and two ahead of Ryder Cup hero Padraig Harrington. Stephen repeated the round on the second day and made the cut comfortably despite the constant threat of a thunderstorm which eventually exploded onto the course and forced tournament officials to reduce the event to 54 holes.

Now he could concentrate on making money, which would be certain to test his new mental skills as he came down the stretch, aware as he always was that a single missed putt could cost him more cash than a nurse earns in a year.

Stephen was ready.

He discussed his opening two rounds with his caddy, Irishman Dermot Byrne, over a beer in the clubhouse. They concluded that his game was good, excellent in fact, and that he was capable of 'shooting the lights out' and recording a really low total.

Stephen started the final round disappointingly with two bogeys in the first four holes - then it happened. He birdied five of the next six holes to go out in 34. He went on to birdie the 10th, eagle the 15th and birdie the 16th and 17th before parring the 18th to finish with 65, seven-under-par or rather nine-under-par for 14 holes. He had taken 25 putts and his average drive had improved from 293 yards in the first round to 313 yards in the final round.

"I was two-over after four but I was determined to stick with my new routine," Stephen says. "I hadn't shot nine-under for 14 holes for years not since I was an amateur. It came right out of the blue. I wasn't thinking about my score, just the target, my routine, my zone and hitting the ball."

Stephen's finishing total was 13-under-par and just six shots behind the champion Ian Poulter, who blew everyone away in the first round with an incredible 61. Stephen picked up £13,000, his highest cheque for 19 tournaments. He finished 10th, his highest finish for almost a year, but more importantly his success had proved to him that the old Stephen had gone forever. And he wasn't coming back.

"It's so simple yet I'd never done it before," says Stephen, looking back. "It was like a light being switched on. On the range we started concentrating on targets and good shots that I'd hit sometime in the past, shots that were important at the time. I felt brilliant when I chipped in in Madrid, so I thought about that and the difference was amazing. In fact I just couldn't hit a bad shot on the range.

"Before that, on the first tee all my thoughts were about technique and if I played badly I'd try something else, then something else - but nothing worked. A lot of Tour players think like that.

"If I had hit the ball badly on the range, I would be worried on the first tee. Now it doesn't matter to me. I just go on the tee and hit it - I don't worry any more.

"Confidence can go in two shots if you're thinking of technique. I had got into the habit of thinking negatively - 'let's just get it off the tee, let's hit it away from the trouble' - that's the sort of thing I'd say to myself. Now I just think of the shot in front of me and where I want the ball to go. Your parameters come right in and if you hit a bad shot it will be 10 yards off line, not 50."

Stephen's improvement continued towards the end of the year and into the early part of the following season, most notably in the Heineken Classic at Royal Melbourne.

He finished fourth, with a four-round total of 12-under-par, and earned £28,000, one of the highest paycheques of his nine-year career. He had many reasons to celebrate, especially his magnificent final round of 65, seven-under-par and the lowest round of the day.

"I've always felt that I'm a better player than my results suggest and that I have a lot of potential," he says. "I knew all about the zone, but that only happened to me every now and then.

"But now, thanks to John, I'm in the zone every time I play. John has taught me how to think like that all the time, even if I'm not hitting the ball well. Now, when I get over the ball I just think of my target. My goal is to get into contention every week.

"Tiger Woods is the best in the world mentally. He's been doing that since he was 12 years old. Every Tour player can hit good shots but with Tiger, well, under pressure, every time he goes out he expects to win.

"His routine is perfect, his swing is perfect and he's athletic. But he's also the best mentally and that's no coincidence. It makes him the best in the world. What really separates him from the rest are his mental strength and his routine. He doesn't think about things over the ball.

"If I had played with Tiger before I met John, I would probably have tried too hard and I'd end up forcing shots. I'd probably be working on my swing out there on the course, too. Now I think I could cope. I would just go through my routine. Yes, I would be nervous. Who wouldn't? Even Woods gets nervous, but it's all about channelling your feelings the right way."

The change in the way Stephen views his career and future prospects has been spectacular. And there is powerful and conclusive numerical evidence published by the European Tour press office which makes pleasant reading as he ponders the new season.

Stephen's stroke average had improved from the previous year from 72.61 (143rd) to 70.86 (80th), which is the best part of a seven-shot reduction per tournament, which is the difference between a Ferrari and a Ford Focus and means he could seriously contemplate contending and ultimately winning tournaments.

There are other encouraging changes throughout his game, including a seven-yard increase in driving distance. But the most revealing statistic is Stephen's incredible improvement in driving accuracy, such a vital component of low scores.

Professional golfers who miss fairways do not make sufficient money. They miss more greens, find more bunkers, take more putts and end up contemplating a dramatic career change selling motor cars or peddling double glazing.

With the help of John Pates, Stephen has increased his driving accuracy from 62.2 per cent (71st) to 78.1 per cent (fifth), which means he is hitting two more fairways every round, enabling him to record fewer bogeys and more birdies.

"I was stuck in a rut and I obviously wanted to get in contention and win a tournament. But I was getting in my own way. Now my technique has improved thanks to my coach Adam Hunter. I'm focused now but I wasn't then and I knew it was all down to the mental game. The trouble was I didn't know who to see.

"I remember asking all the top guys on the Tour how important they thought the mental game was to them and they all said it was a really big factor. Open champion Paul Lawrie has worked on his mind for the last five years and he told me it was pivotal to his success. I started thinking to myself that I had never done that so there must be something wrong.

"I've always had people telling me that I should be winning and there's nothing worse because that puts pressure on you. I don't want to be one of those guys who could have done better. I know now I might hit the ball in the rough or in the trees. Everyone does. What is important is how I react to it.

"I've got just five GCEs and before I met John I found all this stuff Double Dutch. I tried reading psychology books but it all went over my head. Now things are looking good and I can't wait for the season to start."

When Stephen looks back at how he used to be, chasing the perfect swing, focusing on out- of-bounds fences and pot bunkers, he smiles to himself, looking ahead to all the low scores he's going shoot and all the money he's going to accumulate, as if he can't quite believe life could ever be quite this good.

How I work with Elite Golfers

Tour players like Stephen Gallacher come to sports psychologists for one thing – to get into the zone. The trouble is they don't know how to get there. Every now and then they'll shoot a low score but they lack consistency. So they come to me to find out what the zone is, how it works and how to tap into it, so they can transform normal levels of accomplishment.

Professional golfers know if they get in the zone they are more likely to play well, perhaps even win a European Tour tournament, but their needs are exactly the same as the requirements of high handicappers - it's just that their goals and expectations are different. Stephen Gallacher wants to win a European Tour event and earn the £150,000 cheque that might go with it, whereas a club golfer wants to cut his handicap or win the monthly medal. Either way they won't fulfill their potential without getting in the zone more often.

So what is the zone? Well, there are lots of factors and every golfer will have experienced them many times but usually by accident. You'll find yourself in the zone, without warning, usually after hitting a good shot. It will enable you to play well, probably superbly. It might last one shot or one hole, and if you're lucky it could continue for a week but one thing is certain. You'll fall out of your zone and you won't know how to get back in.

When a player is in the zone he does not think about technical thoughts, and most importantly he'll be having fun. The player will experience high levels of energy and feelings of power and he will be in complete control. He is calm, mentally and physically, and he'll be overwhelmed by a feeling of confidence. Players are not all the same though. Some experience what I call 'calm aggression,' so they are on a high when they are in the zone and they need high levels of stimulation to play their best. That kind of player is not common, though. Most of us play better when we reduce the pressure and experience calm.

A Tour player can usually get into the zone after he has hit a particularly good shot. They are all looking for one great shot which will allow them to experience positive feelings which often enables the player to put together a string of birdies. You see this time and time again on the leaderboards on the Tour around the world. And there's a reason for it.

Good shots are associated with certain emotions. But players get things the wrong way round. If they learnt how to access the emotions first they'd hit more good shots and shoot lower scores.

When I first met Stephen Gallacher he told me he hadn't been playing well for some time. The week before, in Madrid, he had just scraped enough money to keep his Tour card for the following season. There had been a recent bereavement in the family so he wasn't feeling too good, which was, of course, understandable.

We started talking about what went on in his mind when he played his best. We worked out a pre-shot routine which allowed him to experience the kind of emotions he felt when he was in his zone. We called it 'his bubble.'

Firstly we had to remove all technical thoughts when he is on the course, especially in a tournament and even more especially when he is actually swinging the club. Stephen was a great pupil who had faith in our plan.

Stephen's old pre-shot routine involved a set of movements that was designed to aim him correctly at the target - you've all read the books, everything square to the line - clubhead, feet, hips and shoulders. That's great but he wasn't aiming his mind.

If you asked a taxi driver to take you to a house in Birmingham, he might get within 20 or 30 miles of your destination but you would never arrive without telling him the area, street and number. Well, your mind is the same. You have to get your mind to line up with the target as well as your body and clubface.

Stephen started to focus really hard on his target, whether it was the pin or a particular spot on the fairway he wanted the ball to finish. He took a snapshot of the image as if he had a mental camera inside his head that froze the scene so he could access a still, colour photograph clearly in his mind. So when he looked away from the target and back at the ball he would see the target clearly in his mind.

That mental picture forced out all the other thoughts that had prevented him from playing his best. This made it impossible for Stephen to think about outcomes, bad shots or technical thoughts, all the things that had paralysed him before and made him miss nine cuts from 11 tournaments.

All those feelings can destroy you. Evaluation and concentrating on technique instead of mental pictures is what is known as 'left brain activity.' The left side of your brain controls language, evaluation and problem solving. Of course, golfers don't know this, but they need to recognise that it is impossible to get in the zone unless you stop thinking this way.

The right side of the brain is all about art, creativity and is based on imagery. This is what you should be using to play golf and is the reason geniuses like Seve Ballesteros and Lee Trevino have been so successful. They are artists.

So how can we achieve that? It would be great if we had a switch on the side of our heads so we could turn from one to another, like clicking from AM to FM on your radio. Obviously we can't do that but if you understand how your brain works, you can learn how to control it, and then you can get in the zone and fulfil your goals.

You use your left brain when you write out a shopping list and when you tick off the tins of beans and biscuits as you place them in your basket. The right brain is all about art, so you use this if you draw or paint or kick a football, anything that is creative.

If you are in a music shop contemplating a CD and you choose Robbie Williams instead of Elton John, that's the left brain. But when you get home and play the album and experience pleasure, that's your right brain.

The right brain controls the rhythm, speed and tempo of motor movements, which happens to be precisely what you are trying to do when you are attempting to hit a golf ball.

So if you can shift activity to the right brain you are much more likely to make a better swing, a better contact and a better shot. But that's not all, you will 'quiet' the part of your mind that could make you worry about out of bounds or lakes or the cash you might lose to your partners if you don't hole that five-foot putt. The left brain creates anxiety.

We define our emotions and our world through language. So if you shut down language it is impossible to worry. You can't think to yourself 'my swing is terrible' or 'these clubs are not good for me.' Shut down your left brain and you will throw away all the stuff that creates problems in every sport.

Tour players are the same as club golfers. When they play badly it is almost always because they think badly, when they concentrate on technique or when they start to worry about outcomes, such as if they are going to make the cut, how much money it might cost them, or perhaps a bad shot they might have hit earlier in the round in similar circumstances.

Thinking of bad shots will kill you. That will make you think negatively, and then you'll hit another bad shot, then another and another. Your game is finished.

So how does the handicap player use this information to improve his game? Well, when he is trying to solve a technical problem, say for example his takeaway or the position at the top of his backswing, he should think of images too. I'm not saying we don't need coaches, just that the way we think is just as important. Stop using language and gimmicks from golf magazines and start focusing on images. Perhaps think of yourself as Tiger Woods, hitting the ball. That would be a start.

See it in your mind and try to copy it. This way of thinking is in conjunction with a coach, not instead of him. You have a mind for playing and a mind for practise. You have to go to a good coach to improve and you need a Sports Psychologist to help you control the emotions and thoughts which can help get into these bubbles, to get in the zone. Then you'll play well more often, get your handicap down and take the cash off you pals on a Sunday morning.

As I've said before, Tour players and 18-handicappers have many things in common. They do the same things wrong. Most of their problems come when they are over the ball, and they get distracted, and start thinking of their family, the out-of-bounds fence, the lake, or opening the clubface on the backswing.

Either way they'll get the same results - bad shots. So the 18-handicapper might slice his shot out of bounds or thin his approach but the professional player will miss a green or a putt and end up shooting 73, which isn't much good on the Tour. If he continues to think that way he'll miss the cut, earn no money and lose his card.

They each need a way to access the zone more often so that it isn't just an accident. The best way to do this is to create an image inside your head of exactly what you are trying to do, whether it's holing a putt or hitting a two-iron over a lake to a tight pin 220 yards away. Think about success, see it in you mind, especially over the ball.

You stare at the flag, come back to the ball and see the image of the flag in your mind. It could be a moving image, a video of the flag fluttering in the breeze or it can be a still image, a photograph in your mind. Your brain reacts to what you put into to it. If you put in a bad shot your brain will create a bad shot, if you put in a target, your brain will mobilise all its resources to get that ball to the target.

When you practice you must split your session evenly. One shot should be on whatever technical aspect you are trying to improve. You should follow this with a mental rehearsal of your pre-shot routine, and focus on a picture of the target in your mind. Seeing the target clearly works for EVERY player I have ever worked with. If the target is clear they hit a better shot than if it is fuzzy.

You will achieve this if you work on what psychologists refer to as sub-modalities. I'll explain this in a later section. One final thought that will help all players - relive a great shot you have played. That was the mental key Fred Couples used throughout his career.

Jack Nicklaus often said that he 'went to the movies' which meant he saw video footage of the perfect shot in his mind before he actually hit the ball. I know many people find this hard so the next best thing is to visualise a great shot you've actually played yourself and the more detail you give to the memory the more successful you will be. This will give you the buzz and the high that will put you in a bubble. You must bombard your mind with good shots.

You don't have to be a pro to have experienced that. We've all hit dozens of good shots at some time in the past, whatever our level of ability. It could be a drive or a birdie or a hole in one. Anything. Even a 24-handicapper has hit plenty of great shots. That's why he keeps going back.

We all want to get into the zone more often - the main way to do this is imagery. It will take time but when it comes the magic will start. That's what Stephen Gallacher used to shoot nine-under for 14 holes. It will help your clients, too.

Imagery

Mental imagery involves more than just seeing or visualizing. Mental imagery involves experiencing all of the senses - seeing, hearing, smelling, feeling, and tasting. Along with these sensations, you may also experience emotions, moods, and other alternative states of mind. Mental imagery is a technique that programs the human mind to respond as programmed.

This is the key to many of the psychological problems performers have, and an ability to produce clear images of performing is essential for anyone with real aspirations.

The sub-modalities of imagery

Imagery can be increased or decreased by changing the way an image is viewed - the way you see, hear, and experience your imagery.

Below is a list of things you can change. We call these sub-modalities.

Color	Speed	Weight
Distance	Stereo/Mono	Duration
Focus	Volume	Texture
Frame	Tone	Shape
Movement	Size	Pressure
Definition	Brightness	Others
Depth	Dimension	
Sound	Contrast	
Location	Temperature	

Mental imagery can be used as practice, to establish a goal, to warm-up, to improve self-confidence, to enhance concentration, to restructure past disasters, to create mood, positive thoughts, and feelings, to control anxiety, to relax and problem solve, and to achieve other desired outcomes. This is a very powerful technique. START NOW.

You can evaluate your client's imagery ability by having them complete the following exercises.

Choose a moment in your life you enjoyed; a particular experience you had that was inspirational would be a good example. You are to imagine the general situation and provide as much detail from your imagination as possible to make the image just as real as you can. Then rate your imagery on four dimensions:

1. How vividly you saw or visualized the image.
2. How clearly you heard the sounds.
3. How vividly you felt your body movements during the activity.
4. How clearly you were aware of your state of mind or mood or felt the emotions of the situation.

After they have completed imagining the situation in every detail, get them to rate the four dimensions of imagery by circling the number that best describes the image they had.

1. = no image present.
2. = not clear or vivid.
3. = moderately clear and vivid image.
4. = clear and vivid image.
5. = extremely clear and vivid image.

Practicing alone

Select one specific skill at competitions you wish to improve. Now imagine performing the activity at the place where you normally perform the activity without anyone else present. Close your eyes for a moment and try to see yourself at this place - hear the sounds, feel your body perform, and be aware of your state of mind or mood.

a.   Rate how you saw yourself perform the activity.

      1   2   3   4   5

b.   Rate how you heard the sounds of doing the activity.

      1   2   3   4   5

c.   Rate how you felt yourself making the movement.

      1   2   3   4   5

d.   Rate how well you were aware of mood.

      1   2   3   4   5

Practicing with others

Imagine doing the same activity but now you are practicing the skill with significant others around you.

a.   Rate how you saw yourself perform the activity.

      1   2   3   4   5

b.   Rate how you heard the sounds of doing the activity.

      1   2   3   4   5

c.   Rate how you felt yourself making the movement.

      1   2   3   4   5

d.   Rate how well you were aware of mood.

      1   2   3   4   5

Imagine watching yourself perform at your best

a.   Rate how you saw yourself perform the activity.

     1 2 3 4 5

b.   Rate how you heard the sounds of doing the activity.

     1 2 3 4 5

c.   Rate how you felt yourself making movements.

     1 2 3 4 5

d.   Rate how well you were aware of your mood.

     1 2 3 4 5

Construct an image that relaxes you

a.   Rate how you saw yourself perform the activity.

     1 2 3 4 5

b.   Rate how you heard the sounds of doing the activity.

     1 2 3 4 5

c.   Rate how you felt yourself making movements.

     1 2 3 4 5

d.   Rate how well you were aware of mood.

     1 2 3 4 5

Construct psyching-up images

a.   Rate how you saw yourself perform the activity.

      1   2   3   4   5

b.   Rate how you heard the sounds of doing the activity.

      1   2   3   4   5

c.   Rate how you felt yourself making the movement.

      1   2   3   4   5

d.   Rate how well you were aware of mood.

      1   2   3   4   5

Scoring

Total the score for the four rating dimensions 'a' and 'b' and 'c' and 'd' to obtain a total score and record it where indicated.

Situation	Score
a. Visual	_____
b. Auditory	_____
c. Kinaesthetic	_____
d. Mood	_____

A score greater than 15 on each dimension shows that your client has a high level of ability. If your client scores less than 15, they should enhance their imagery ability by completing the 'Imagery Techniques' exercises that follow.

Imagery Techniques

Vividness exercises using sub-modalities

Choose a player you admire and visualize in detail. Focus on their facial features, mannerisms, body build, shape, clothes, tonality of voice, smell, and emotions you feel when you see that person and how he or she makes you feel. Intensify the feeling by using the sub-modalities above.

Imagery Technique One

1. Close your eyes and imagine yourself in a room.
2. Sit down comfortably and visualize a TV in the room.
3. On that TV visualize Tiger Woods.
4. Watch him play shots.
5. Flash words on the screen that describes his game.

Imagery Technique Two

1. Close your eyes and imagine yourself in a room.
2. Sit down comfortably and visualize a TV in the room.
3. On that TV visualize Tiger Woods.
4. Watch him play shots.
5. Flash words on the screen that describes his game.
6. Get out of your chair and step into the screen.
7. Walk up to Tiger and go inside his body.
8. Imagine what it feels like to walk, think and play like Tiger Woods.
9. Imagine swinging the club, imagine putting and chipping during a competition.
10. Focus on the positive attitudes Tiger has such as "hole every shot".
11. Imagine what it is like to win a tournament. Walking down the 18th. Submitting your winning score card and holding the trophy as you give your winning speech.
12. Flash on the TV words that describe how you feel when you win.

Other Performance Enhancing Imagery Techniques

Sensory Dissociation Techniques

Sensory dissociation techniques are useful for dissociating the client from any traumatic feelings associated with memories that lie at the source of a client's problems. Because dissociation is a part of everyday life, especially in experiences such as shock, most people can imagine seeing themselves as if they are looking at themselves as another person.

The great Jack Nicklaus would use this technique as part of his pre-shot routine.

Dissociation removes the client dramatically from the scene of the stress and often a change can occur in one session.

How to create a Dissociative State

As a general rule of thumb you want to help your client's associate with good memories and dissociate from bad memories. When you use this technique, you (the practitioner) may ask the client to imagine a disturbing scenario on a cinema screen. The client is then asked to see themselves sitting in the cinema watching the cinema screen (second position). They are then asked to see themselves from another position (third position) usually in the projection booth. The client is then asked to watch themself, watching themself on the screen going through the experience that is traumatic. When you use this kind of imagery, the client is completely dissociated and is free of the uncomfortable kinaesthetic response that is normally associated with the memory.

By dissociating the client to an observational position, it is possible to 'watch' without negative feelings and learn that is possible to remember the experience with out feeling uncomfortable. This new learning can be very powerful and is often carried over into everyday life and more specifically, into the situation in which the stress occurs.

Exercise - The VK Dissociation Structure.

1. Induce trance

2. Ask the unconscious mind to see the younger self immediately prior to the trauma projected as a still picture on a cinema screen.

3. Ask the unconscious mind to find a resource that will stop the trauma and anchor it by touching the right shoulder.

4. Ask the client to float out of body into the projection booth and see the self, sitting in the cinema.

5. Anchor the dissociation by touching the left shoulder.

6. Ask the client to squeeze their hand if they are traumatised by the images.

7. Get the client to watch themselves in the cinema watching - themselves on the screen in black and white.

8. At the end of the movie get the client to associate with the self on the screen and run the movie backwards in colour.

9. Dissociate the client back to the projection booth and re-run -the movie in colour at normal speed re-associating with the self each time it is run. It is important to give the client time to accomplish this particular exercise.

The Swish Technique

There is a definite cause and effect relationship between the recollection of an unpleasant memory and the associated feelings. Usually the picture is the pre-requisite to the feeling. The mental image triggers the unpleasant kinaesthetic responses. Likewise client's feel good when they see a pleasant image.

The Swish Technique involves asking the client to access the suitable resource required to erase or neutralise the negative traumatic memory. The client is first asked to see the behaviour they want to change and then asked to see and feel the positive resource they would like as an alternative. It is assumed that the client can already see and feel the negative feeling. If the client does not have access to the picture responsible for the negative feeling then a different therapeutic approach should be applied.

The first step involves the client in accessing the picture of the bad memory and its associated feelings and seeing and experiencing this bad memory in an associated state. The client has to step into the image of the memory and experience it as if he were there. The previously accessed positive resource required to neutralise or erase the bad memory should be in the form of a dissociated picture in the distance. The practitioner then asks the client to enlarge the dissociated resource picture bringing it forwards and whilst doing so to push away the associated negative picture. As the positive picture and the negative picture meet and superimpose over one another, so the positive element of the resourceful picture erases or neutralises the negative picture. Simultaneously the associated feelings also superimpose and integrate.

This swishing process also swishes on a kinaesthetic level. The positive feelings from the resourceful picture neutralise the negative feelings from the negative picture so that the client has difficulty in re-accessing the original negative feelings. Usually the client has difficulty in reaccessing the negative image also. As client's rely on their internal images of reference in order to make decisions in the future, the new swished image and related feeling replaces the earlier negative feeling and image as a form of reference. When the client approaches similar events in the future there is only a neutral response.

Exercise

1. Close your eyes and identify a behaviour you want to change and visualise the moment prior to the behaviour you want to change.

2. Attempt to feel as if you are actually there in the experience (be Associated). You should notice an uncomfortable feeling associated with this picture.

3. Create a positive outcome picture of yourself doing what you would rather do as an alternative to the negative behaviour. See yourself in the picture - be disassociated.

4. See the negative picture big and bright in front of you and put the positive picture into a small space in the bottom corner of the negative picture.

5. Now do the Swish by enlarging and swishing the small positive picture up behind and through the negative picture whilst pushing the negative picture away so that the positive picture replaces the negative picture. You should discover that you shift from associated to disassociated as the positive picture swishes through the negative.

6. Open and close your eyes to "break state" and repeat the above swish several times opening and closing the eyes between each swish..

7. Test - open your eyes and try and remember the old negative picture. If the old negative picture still brings up negative feelings, repeat the exercise.

Self-Talk

Performance is not random; it is related to thoughts, expectations and self-talk, as well as physical and technical preparation.

Learning to control self-talk can help golfers manage the information they are feeding themselves on a regular basis. golfers need to make sure self-talk is directed toward improving performance. Just as golfers regularly train their bodies to execute precise skills or maintain a certain body type, they need to regularly train the mind to think precise thoughts and focus on specific things.

Researchers have found that elite golfers use self-talk as a motivational strategy to augment skill acquisition, to control focus, to enhance self-confidence, and to control emotions. All of these factors have a profound affect on performance.

The type of self-talk generated by the golfer will, to a large extent, determine whether performance is improved or impaired. Studies that have looked at the effect of positive, negative, and neutral self-talk on performance, indicate that participants in the positive self-talk group outperformed those in the negative and neutral self-talk groups. Additionally, researchers have also found negative self-talk to be linked with diminished performance.

Self-talk includes all the things said both silently and out loud. Self-talk can be positive; it can tell an golfer what to do, where to focus, and get them motivated ("You can do it"). Unfortunately, self talk can also be negative ("You're not good enough, so just give it up"), pessimistic, and critical. Such internal talk does not help performance and, in most cases, probably hurts performance. Recognize that negative self-talk is going to occur; the key is to not focus on the negatives and instead focus on the positives.

Performance is hindered when golfers worry about what **may** happen ("I may hit that shot into the bunker"). All you have control over is **right now:** that is where thoughts need to be.

Similarly not 'letting go' of mistakes or poor performances takes thoughts and focus away from the present.

There are common self-talk errors people make that tend to have a negative influence on performance. Using the following scale, read through each of these 'thoughts' and assess if any of these errors effect you.

Strongly Agree   Strongly Disagree

    1   2   3   4   5

Focusing on the past or future:

Example

"I can't believe I missed that opportunity."

Do you engage in this type of self-talk?

Strongly Agree   Strongly Disagree

    1   2   3   4   5

Not 'letting go' of past mistakes or poor performances, takes thoughts and focus away from the present.

A similar situation occurs when people focus on what they are trying to avoid and not what they want to happen.

Focusing on weaknesses:

Example
"The people I play with are always better than me."

Do you engage in this type of self-talk?

Dwelling on weaknesses will erode confidence. Ideally, you should focus on strengths such as: "I have always been great at inspiring people."

Focusing only on outcome:

Example
"I must achieve this target."

"I must make more money."

Do you engage in this type of self-talk?

Strongly Agree   Strongly Disagree

    1   2   3   4   5

These thoughts direct you to the outcome, something you have little control over. What golfers do have control over is performance. Therefore, direct self-talk towards what needs to be done (such as focusing on creating a playful and positive working environment) and trust that the outcome will take care of itself.

Focusing on uncontrollable factors:

Example

"I don't like the way she talks to me."

Do you engage in this type of self-talk?

Strongly Agree   Strongly Disagree

| 1 | 2 | 3 | 4 | 5 |

Statements such as these are a waste of mental energy. Not only are they out of your control, but they also distract thoughts from where you should be. Keep thoughts on controllable factors, such as these:

Your strengths:

People strengths.

Improving mental toughness.

Emotions.

Consistency.

Punctuality.

Diet.

Enjoyment.

What you think (Thoughts-feelings-behaviour).

What you say to yourself.

What you say to others.

Who you listen to.

Guidelines about Self-Talk

The following six simple rules:

Rule one: Avoid thoughts that lead to worry or anxiety.

Golfers who perform inconsistently, especially those who perform poorly in the face of risk and pressure, have self-talk which is centered on being afraid (afraid of losing, afraid of letting others down) or on doubting their ability ("I can't do it…I haven't trained enough."). Such statements must be avoided. Statements of doubt or fear erode confidence and generate stress.

Rule two: Avoid thinking about past failures.

Thinking about your failures will create a negative thought process and it is likely to create high stress. If you have an event at a site where you experienced a particularly disappointing experience, keep your mind away from replaying that past event. Reviewing past failures prior to an important and current event will increase stress and lower the chance of your performing at your best level.

Rule three: Avoid thinking that ties self-worth to performance.

Avoid statements which imply that your self-esteem will be damaged by poor performance. Internal dialogue statements that indicate this error, are ones such as, "If I miss this opportunity, I'm not any good" or "If I don't make this cut, it's because I'm worthless." When a person has the attitude that winning contracts is critical for maintaining self-esteem, the stakes are too high. Unnecessary stress is generated and it will affect performance.

Rule four: Monitor your internal dialogue.

To change internal dialogue, monitor what you say to yourself prior to and during meetings or presentations.

Rule five: Regard stress symptoms in a positive way.

Stress reactions are open to interpretation. You can view competitive stress positively, when you regard stress as exciting and challenging. Rather than saying to yourself, "I'm afraid" or "I feel weak and shaky with nerves," re-interpret the symptoms. Say to yourself, "I feel challenged; I feel powerful; I feel excited; I'm ready." Such statements help you to shift the interpretation of stress to a feeling of being psyched up and challenged. Interestingly, Tiger Woods and Jack Nicklaus viewed competitive stress as exciting and what they practiced for.

Rule six: Convert negative statements into positive ones.

The person who brings your attention to 'mistakes' may create problems. This directive increases your chances of making an error. Tell yourself what you want to make happen rather than what you wish to avoid.

As a general guideline for self-talk, use two types of statements: encouraging statements and instructional statements. Encouraging statements bolster confidence. "You can do it," "You're good," "You're a champ," are examples of this type of inner dialogue. Self-talk that focuses attention on performance skills and your strengths provides the other positive form of internal dialogue.

Consistent application of these guidelines creates new habits in inner dialogue that gives players greater control over performance.

Concentration

"I was blessed with the ability to focus intensely on whatever I'm doing through most distraction and usually, to the exclusion of whatever else might otherwise preoccupy me."

- Jack Nicklaus -

Most professional golfers would agree that concentration is one of the most important skills required to achieve a high level of performance. For golf performance, the results of several studies have suggested that performance improves when attention is directed away from the production of movement.

Focusing our thoughts on the right things can have a dramatic effect on our results. In my consultancy, I get my client's to focus on the things that get them into the zone, such as positive emotions, by using a client–centered approach to create pre-shot routines. The structure of this approach is described below:

Pre-shot and Post-shot Routines

Research and anecdotal evidence tell us that the use of performance routines is perhaps the most effective way of improving the performance of a player. Professional golfers use routines to control their thoughts, emotions and concentration. The great Jack Nicklaus reported he never hit a shot without performing a routine.

Most golfers think a pre-shot routine means one specific gimmick which kick-starts their swing. It could be a waggle, a turn of the head or a distinct movement such as kicking in your knee or pressing your toes together. These things may have moderate benefits if they control your concentration but there's so much more you can do to improve your play.

The purpose of a pre-shot routine should be to get yourself into the right mental state. A good mental pre-shot routine will also assist you to get 'in the zone.'

To try to help you understand the practicalities of my teaching I'm going to tell you about a pre-shot and post routine that helped Darren Clarke win the English Open a couple of years ago. We've talked about this before but the big man's experiences will give you a perfect example of the benefits of thinking correctly, of getting into your zone.

Darren had a terrible round in the Pro-Am the day before the actual tournament. He had fallen into the habit of using his pre-shot routine to focus on bad shots, technique and outcomes – the result was catastrophic – he shot 84. I talked with Darren that evening and we worked out a different way of thinking designed to help him get in his zone. He started relaxing, and began to focus on getting into a high emotional state by recalling how he felt when he played his best. The next day he shot 65, a reduction of 19 shots. It takes some believing, doesn't it?

He went on to win the tournament with a 17-under-par total. We talked for a while after the prize giving and Darren told me that the only time he stopped thinking correctly was on the 17th tee in the final round, when the pressure was at its highest. He hit a poor tee shot into deep rough and he was forced to hack the ball back onto the fairway. The lie was terrible and he had no alternative. His bad tee-shot was a wake-up call so Darren slipped comfortably back into the correct way of thinking, returned into his zone immediately and hit a perfect eight-iron that finished a metre from the flag. He went on to par the 18th and win his first title for almost a year – and all because he used his mind to think the right way before and after every shot.

Your pre-shot and post-shot routines should incorporate mental skills that get you into the right feelings and emotions that will make it more likely for you to get 'in your zone.' If you go out on the golf course and think the right way, you will find your zone most of the time.

Music as an Intervention

The influence of music in the promotion of flow states in sport has been the subject of one of my research interests, with the prevailing view being that carefully selected music may promote flow. Recent publications show music not only can be used to control flow it can also be used to control emotions and the rhythm of a golfers swing. When I worked with Darren Clarke at the English Open, his pre-shot routine involved using the "Eye of the tiger". Similarly Stephen Gallacher won the Dunhill Championships using the music of the Smiths. Sam Snead and Bobby Jones also used music to control emotions and the rhythm of their swings. This is a very powerful technique especially if you use it with best performance imagery. The procedure for using this technique is described below:

1. Ask your client to recall the images and feelings they associate with their experiences of flow in sport.

2. Direct your client to rehearse an image of flow and to imagine performing their golf swing from an internal perspective.

3. After this period of instruction, ask your client to select a single track of music from their own compact disc collection that facilitates feelings similar to the flow experiences they have during performance.

4. Help the client find ways of using music within their pre-shot or post-shot routines.

Autotelic States as an Intervention

In the playful autotelic state, players work harder and are more creative and innovative. Playfulness is the heart of peak performance. In the playful state, players can enthusiastically face important competitions and do not develop fears about failure, success or the unknown. They find competitions rewarding, fun and exciting. On the other side of the coin, players in the serious state are often stricken by anxiety and become quickly demoralized. The greatest gift you can give your clients is the confidence to play in a playful state. This is the secret of many of our great players. This mental state enables players the ability to win under pressure.

Further Action

Thank you for using the practitioners guide. The knowledge in this guide has helped golfers win tournaments all over the world.

New ideas and technologies are developed in this field every day. This is why we have set up a website to keep you up to date with these new developments. The website is also designed to give you advice. This support service is completely free. All you have to do is go online and type in www.bigolfpsychology.com to talk to a chartered golf psychologist.

Lightning Source UK Ltd.
Milton Keynes UK
UKOW021036280413

209890UK00001B/3/P